Big Girls Don't Cry

By Regina Jefferson

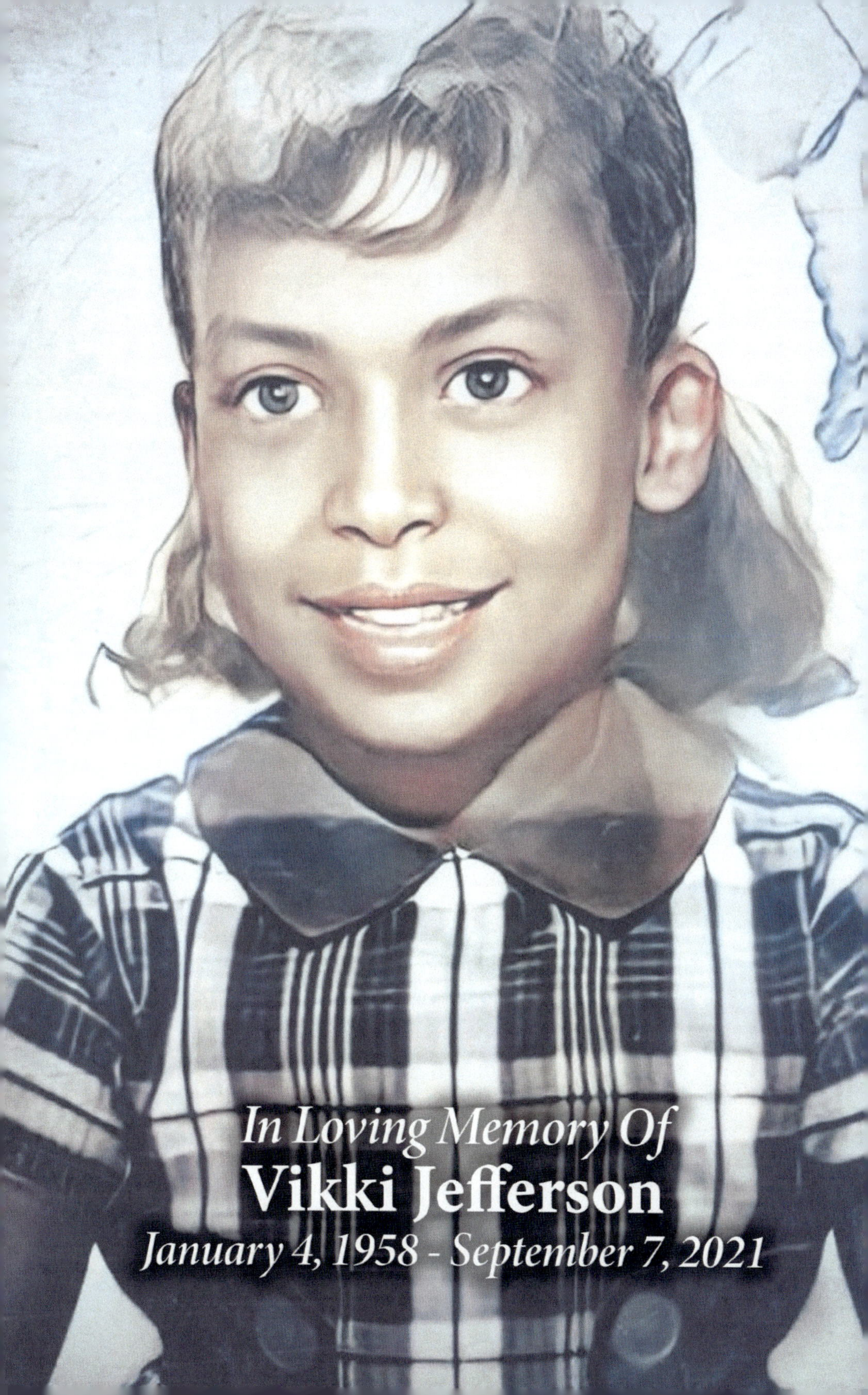
In Loving Memory Of
Vikki Jefferson
January 4, 1958 - September 7, 2021

Big Girls Don't Cry

By Regina "Queen" Jefferson

Big Girls Don't Cry

However, sometimes they cry in other ways,
but they all do cry.

This Book Was Inspired By:

"Big Girls Don't Cry"
"Lift your hands and tell the Lord thank you"
MISSIONARY LULA MAY JEFFERSON
Grandmother

"Sing what I sing, you can do it,
I believe in you"
MISSIONARY MARGIE WHITE
Great Aunt

"Never forget the pleasure of the journey"
VIKKI JEFFERSON
Aunt & Best Friend

"It's not what others do to you,
it's how you respond to them"
MISSIONARY JUANITA DIANE HARPER
Mother

"I'm so happy you're talking about the book.
You can help so many people. I am so proud
of you. Love you sister."
LYNDA HENDERSON
Sister

Table of Contents

CHAPTER 1
Chelle Belle & Big Girl

In 1962, Rachelle ("Chelle") was born in Tulsa, Oklahoma. Her mother, Missionary Juanita Diane Harper called her Chelle. They both moved to Wichita, Kansas, where Chelle's mother later married Chelle's father and started a life in ministry. Because Chelle was her first granddaughter, Chelle's grandmother, Missionary Lula May Jefferson, would come to visit the family weekly; but much to her grandmother's surprise, Chelle would always start to cry whenever she picked Chelle up. When Chelle was a toddler, her grandmother affectionately named her "Chelle Bell" because Chelle wore bells on her shoes, so her mother would know when she was coming since she didn't speak.

Grandmother: "Chelle Bell, would you please stop crying? Big girls don't cry. Don't you know that big girls don't cry? Now, aren't you a big girl?"

Chelle's grandmother was in her early thirties when Chelle was born. Since Chelle's grandmother thought she was too young to be a grandmother and would always say "Big Girl, don't cry" to Chelle, she decided to have Chelle Bell refer to her as Big Girl rather than grandmother. The reason

Chelle's grandmother was such a young grandmother was because Chelle's grandmother was 13 years old when she was violated by her own father and told by her father not to cry; but be a big girl and take on the responsibility of becoming a mother.

Teenage pregnancies can be very challenging for many reasons; therefore, having strong family support and/or the support of faith communities can be beneficial for teenage mothers. When a child or teenager is violated, they should report it to their parents, a family member, an adult or a faith leader they trust. Victims of abuse or violence can also attend group counseling or call the 24/7 National Sexual Assault hotline at 1-800-656-4673.

Chelle was not aware of the painful ordeal her grandmother had experienced and also had no idea that her mother had been born out of wedlock (born to unmarried parents). For Chelle to come along years later and identify her grandmother's pain with the name, Big Girl, was spiritual. When Chelle's sister and brother were born, they also started calling their grandmother "Big Girl."

CHAPTER 2
Chelle The Songstress

Chelle's mother did everything she could to make Chelle speak words, but she was unsuccessful, so she taught Chelle to sing the words as a way of communicating with her. Chelle would continue to use songs as a way of talking to her mom until she turned 5 years old. She would sing these words to her mother.

Chelle: (singing) "Momma, I want some water". "Momma, I love your dearly", "Momma, thank you for loving me", "Momma, I love you dearly!" Chelle loved singing her favorite songs in front of the family.

Chelle: (singing) "I want to live so that God can use me anytime and anywhere."

Chelle would perform in front of her family and at church where her father, Pastor William Harper was the Assistant Pastor and her mother was the youth Choir Director.

Her great Aunt Margie White had a creative way of teaching Chelle how to sing adult songs. Aunt Margie would sing the words and melody, and Chelle would duplicate the sound and voice. This method of teaching was "call and respond."

Aunt Margie: "Come on Chelle, sing this: How great thou art". Chelle sings: "How great thou art".

Aunt Margie: "Chelle, sing, Then sings my soul my savior God to thee", Chelle sings: "Then sings my soul my savior God to thee." "How great thou art, how great thou art".

Aunt Margie encouraged her to sing adult songs, so that she would feel special and talented. Chelle's mother also taught her and her siblings how to sing gospel songs, written for adult singers. This made Chelle feel so special and gifted.

When Chelle and her family would evangelize in front of large audiences, Chelle had no fear of performing in front of a crowd. However, Chelle had a secret that no one knew. She was not a good speller or writer, and she was terrified of reading in front of people. This secret was something she was ashamed of and she feared others would make fun of her.

CHAPTER 3
Chelle's School Days

Chelle loved going to church to sing; but at school, Chelle's classmates would laugh at how she would read and pronounce her words. Her voice would shake and she would always have her head down when she read. Her physical features of having a major overbite that caused her to pronounce her words incorrectly didn't help.

School Children: "Hey Chelle! Bucked tooth beaver, goofy, we're talking to you! What are you looking for on the floor?" (Followed by loud laughter).

All the teasing from the children in school did not make Chelle feel like she was beautiful. She felt bad about the color of her skin as it was darker than some of the other children's skin. She would speak with her head down and was too embarrassed to smile. She felt bad about her overbite and her two bucked teeth. Because she looked different than everyone else, Chelle did not think she was as beautiful or smart as the other children. Fortunately, when Chelle went to modeling school, the teacher recommended that she go to the dentist to request porcelain veneers. The veneers were actually the solution to Chelle's overbite. Once Chelle's teeth were aligned, she

was no longer ashamed of her smile. However, Chelle still felt insecure about her poor writing skills and feared reading out loud in front of people.

Grade schoolteacher: "When I ask you to read or turn in your grammar paper, it has so many mistakes on it. Chelle, you are a horrible speller and writer. You don't take your time and study. Therefore, you're not a good reader, or writer; I will have to give you a "D" in my class." Chelle had very low self-esteem because of her past experiences with reading out loud in front of people and what her teacher had said to her. Thus, when Chelle had to read, her stomach would turn upside down and her hands would sweat. Her heart would beat fast, making it hard to breathe, all because of the thought of her reading in front of her elementary classroom or at Sunday school.

She would get sick; and later in life, develop irritable bowel syndrome due to the worry and stress of what she thought about herself. Eventually, a holistic doctor informed Chelle she had a vitamin defiency and suggested she try B complex because it is good for the nervous system. Thankfully, taking the B complex eased the symptoms of Chelle's condition.

Because Chelle had been so afraid of what others would say, she had never told anyone about how she felt about others teasing and making fun of her until she went to therapy.

If you are being teased, please tell your teacher, school counselor, faith leader or family members immediately. You may also contact the Crisis/Bullying Crisis Text line 741741 or STOP BULLYING NOW HOTLINE 1-800-273-8255.

CHAPTER 4
Chelle Gains Her Confidence

Chelle's low self-esteem caused her to get into trouble in school. She was sent to Passport to Adventure, a wilderness therapy program for troubled youth. At this point, she realized she had to make a major change in her life. Receiving the Lord and living a life with Christ helped Chelle discover her true purpose. If you have not accepted the Lord and Savior Jesus Christ into your life, please consider doing so as a relationship with Jesus Christ may help you discover your true purpose, as it did with Chelle.

At church, Chelle had one Sunday school teacher, Sister Patricia Jones, who believed in Chelle and encouraged her to have faith in her abilities. Sister Jones would always encourage Chelle to keep working on her reading and told her she would get better. Chelle decided to stop crying about what she wasn't good at and use the gift of singing for reading and singing for communicating.

Chelle would practice in front of a mirror. Then she started reading in front of her family and friends. Chelle performed funny shows and stories she wrote. This helped to boost her confidence about reading in front of others.

When Chelle turned 18 years old, she decided to go to college to take classes in mass communication and acting to gain more confidence in reading and speaking in public. When she was able to act out the words, she could hide behind her fears and become the character; therefore, giving her confidence to read and speak in front of any size audience. She received an "A+" in these courses. She loved speaking on the radio, and soon became a radio celebrity hostess.

For the first time in her life, she was not afraid. However, she secretly was still not a good speller or a writer. She had to find a way to overcome her fears. One day, a sister friend gave her advice about how to address her fears.

Patrice (Sister/Friend): "Chelle, you're an excellent speaker, why don't you write the way you speak and have someone edit what you write? Although I am a good writer, I always have someone edit what I write."

Chelle decided to take the advice of her sister/friend. She made a conscious decision to speak everything out loud, before she would write. This technique helped change her writing and spelling forever.

Years later during her sisterhood luncheon with her sisters, Charis and T'Wana, something magical happened.

Charis told her, "When you change what you tell yourself about your abilities, your abilities will change." T'Wana told her, "When you write, pray and ask God to help you with your wording. It helped me after my stroke. I was having problems with writing, and I prayed to God to help me with my wording, and he helped me to regain my ability to write. I still always have someone look over my writing."

Chelle told her sisters, "I have never been a good writer or speller. Everyone has something they're not good at, and well, mine is spelling and writing!"

The moment with her sisters was a turning point for Chelle. She looked up to her sisters and their abilities in writing. Chelle had always told herself and others that she was not a good writer. She used the excuse of not being a good writer to justify her fears when talking with her sisters. Chelle determined within herself that moving forward, it was time for her to change her self-talk.

For the first time in a long while, Chelle decided to stop crying about something she did not believe was possible. She dried up her tears and started believing she would be a good writer and speller. She decided that day to start speaking life over her self and her abilities. She prayed and asked God to help her with her fears.

Every day, she would look in the mirror and say, "I am a good writer. I am a good speller, and I am a good speaker." She took several writing classes and had all of her writing edited, just as her sister friend suggested.

CHAPTER 5
Chelle's Career

Chelle would later move from Wichita, Kansas to Kansas City, Missouri where she worked on national radio stations. After she graduated from college, she got a job working on the radio where she read and spoke on national and international platforms. She used her talent to perform in theaters and sing on stages. Who would believe she didn't start speaking until the age of five?

Chelle hosted her own live call-in talk show for over 10 years. She also worked at TV stations as a reporter. Then in 2001 at the age of 40, she moved to Washington, D.C. from Kansas City, Missouri. She has been a talk show host on national and international TV and radio for 30 years.

At the age of 44, Chelle interviewed the first African-American man who became the President of the United States of America, Barack Obama. She traveled to Africa and spoke in front of tribal Kings and Queens of Abuja and Lagos, Nigeria. She was featured on radio in 36 states, and in Africa where her interviews were translated into other languages.

Chelle was a teacher for Dale Carnegie's national 16-week

courses to teach students how to build their confidence in personal leadership. In addition, Chelle interviewed national and international celebrities on WOL and XM radio stations in Washington, D.C. In 2012, she received the Community Choice Award from DCTV channel 16 for the Best Community Health and Wellness show in the District of Columbia, Maryland and Virginia areas. She has been a featured soloist on several musical CD's, a Podcast host, a spiritual coach and the CEO for Speak Life LLC.

Chelle was featured in two movies: "Bound and Gagged", where she played a Bishop's wife, a role which brought awareness to domestic violence and "Eboni Love" where she played the role of a Counselor in an internet movie focused on relationships; and now, you're currently reading Chelle's first children's book entitled: "Big Girls Don't Cry!"

CHELLE'S CHALLENGE

The challenge to you, dear reader, is to determine what you think are limitations in your life and to use them as stepping stones for your next purpose in life. Speak life over your weakness and become the greatest version of yourself. The world needs you! Never forget the pleasure of your life's journey. Your fears and your pain can become your purpose.

BOUND & GAGGED
THE STAGE PLAY, THE MISSION, THE MINISTRY
great day
WASHINGTON
wusa 9

SHANNON WHREN'S
BOUND AND GAGGED
A TRUE STORY OF DOMESTIC VIOLENCE
REGINA JEFFERSON AS
"MOTHER STELLA"
BRADE EUBANKS
AS
"BISHOP MCDANIEL"

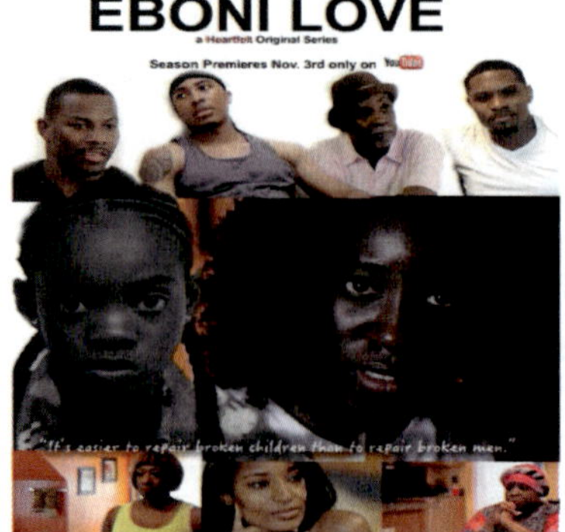
EBONI LOVE
Season Premieres Nov. 3rd only on YouTube

A "special thank you" to the following people who were instrumental in helping my journey of fear and self-doubt turn into a life of purpose.

In Memory Of:
Missionary Juanita Diane Harper (Mother)
Missionary Lula May Jefferson (Grandmother)
Missionary Margie White (Great Aunt)
Missionary Martha Swindall (Great Aunt)
Vikki Jefferson (Aunt and Best Friend)
Betty Redmond (Godmother)
Robin Jackson (Sister Friend)
Lynda Henderson (Sister)

Editors and Trainers:
Baron Bell and Lynda Henderson
Special thanks for helping me to be a better version of myself.

Father and Spiritual Leaders:
Pastor William. L Harper Sr.
Elder William L. Harper Jr.

Sisters and Coaches:
Patrice Bailey, Charis Ferguson, Lynda Henderson,
T'Wana Holmes, Robin Jackson, Rev. Dana Mitchell,
Terrell Powell, Sheryl Harper
and Brenda Ridgnal (Best Friend)

Mentors/Spiritual Mentors:
Dr. Brenda Crowder-Gains
Dr. Sarita Graham
Poet Danny Queen
Evangelist Stephanie Smith and Stephanie Baker

Spiritual Teachers/Friends:
Reginald Lyons, Rev. Darryl Moch, and Kaleef Morse,
Shawn Baker, Brian Anderson,
Rev. Carmi Washington-Flood and Colleen Green

Executive Editors + Creative
Pastor Lewis & Dr. Sharon Johnson
www.C-2.biz

Regina RaChelle's Favorite Scriptures:

Proverbs 3:6

"In all thy ways acknowledge him and he shall direct thy path."

Philippians 4:13

"I can do all things through Christ that strengthens me."

Psalm 34:1

"I will bless the Lord at all times; his praises shall continually be in my mouth."

Big Girls Don't Cry Journal

Question 1: What are you afraid of doing?

____

____

____

____

Question 2: What are your special talents?

____

____

____

____

Question 3: Who is the person that can help you with your fears?

____

____

____

____

Quesiont 5: Who is your favorite person in the world and why?

Question 6: What do you do to make yourself and others happy?

NOTES

NOTES

For Questions, Booking or Contact, Email:
REGINAJEFFERSON@YAHOO.COM

Or log onto:
WWW.SPEAKINGLIFELLC.COM

Made in the USA
Middletown, DE
28 May 2024